Liverpool Fashion

Liverpool Fashion
Its Makers and Wearers

THE DRESSMAKING TRADE IN LIVERPOOL 1830-1940

by Anthea Jarvis
Assistant Keeper of Decorative Arts

Merseyside County Museums

With the exception of Plate 4 and Plate 20,
all photographs reproduced in this book
were taken by Doug Hyslop, Colin Pitcher
David Flower and Ron Boocock,
Photography Department, Merseyside
County Museums.

Designed by
Northern Design Unit, Liverpool

Printed by
Saints & Co. Ltd, Liverpool

Contents

6

Monty P Black FSIAD

I was delighted when Charles Metcalfe of Liverpool Polytechnic
asked me to make a presentation to the costume collections of
the Merseyside County Museums. This was my first introduction
to the Museum and Anthea Jarvis.

It is quite remarkable to reflect on the standard of workmanship
in the costumes held at the Museum and it is doubtful if these
skills could be reproduced today. Yet it is not totally lost;
we are today producing in Liverpool highly intricate designs
for the international fashion market. Indeed the high standards
of the Fashion Department at the Polytechnic perpetuate the
skills.

In these difficult times of recession it is beneficial, and
educational, to look back, and the team at the Museum are
doing a splendid job in keeping us aware of the history of
fashion development in Liverpool. Future fashion designers will
use it for a source of inspiration and it will be an area of
enjoyment for the layman, hopefully for many years. I have every
confidence in the team and am grateful for this opportunity to
contribute in some small way.

M P Black

Baccarat 40 Great Marlborough Street London W1V 1DA Telephone 01-734 2881
Wetherall 6/12 Colquitt Street Liverpool L1 4DF Telephone 051-709 5555
Lewis & Black 6/12 Colquitt Street Liverpool L1 4DF Telephone 051-709 5555

Monty Black is Deputy Chairman and Managing Director of
Baccarat/Wetherall, an international fashion company based in Liverpool.

Chapter 1
Introduction

IT is unfortunate that Merseyside's most prolific female diarist and letter writer of the early 19th century, Miss Ellen Weeton, does not seem to have been in the least fashion conscious, nor was she concerned about recording for posterity the problems she had making or otherwise acquiring a suitable wardrobe for herself, which to us today would be far more interesting than the peculiarities of her various friends, which she writes about at length. That clothes, generally, played as large a part in the female mind, even a cultured and well-educated one, as they do today, is made evident by references to the 'clothes problem' in Jane Austen's letters to her sister Cassandra, *(1)* and neither of those two ladies could be accused of being frivolous or vain. Jane Austen told her sister about the silk mercers and the milliners' shops she visited in London while visiting her brother there, but Miss Weeton, though she stayed for long periods with friends in Liverpool, never mentions a single shopping expedition either to buy items of clothing, or the materials to make them. She did, however, from her own account, *(2)* spend a substantial part of her time sewing, and mending, so one assumes that, like the majority of middle-class ladies in her day, she made her own clothes, and thought them nobody's business but her own.

There would indeed have been little chance of buying any ladies' clothes ready-made in the first quarter of the 19th century. Bonnets and shawls, stockings and perhaps an outdoor cloak in a town the size of Liverpool probably could be purchased 'off the peg', but with regard to other items of dress, it was not until the 1840s that underwear could be bought 'ready made', until the 1880s that blouses and summer cotton dresses could be purchased likewise, and it was not until after the First World War that a lady with any pretension to fashion would wear a 'best dress' that had not been individually made, to her order and her measure. For the whole of the 19th century, therefore, the middle and upper class lady acquired her clothes by one of three ways; she either made them herself, she had them made for her by a dressmaker, or, in the last quarter of the 19th century, she could order them from one of the ladies outfitting establishments in the City Centre, where they would be made to measure in their own workrooms.

As Liverpool itself expanded enormously in the 19th century, so the personnel engaged in the dressmaking industry multiplied, and spread from the town centre into the new residential areas and suburbs. In 1827 *Gore's Directory* lists 77 names under 'Milliners and Dressmakers'; *(3)* a quarter of a century later in 1851 the number is 146; this doubled again sixteen years later to 334, and by 1895 the numbers add up to the impressive total of 1,100, and when one adds to this the numbers of other women who sewed for a living but do not appear in Trade

Directories, for example the girls who worked for the dressmakers, and the large numbers of workroom staff the big dress shops employed, the dress trade must have been by far the biggest source of employment for women (excluding domestic service) in Liverpool at the turn of the century.

Although, by the second half of the 19th century, dressmakers, and the drapers and silk mercers' shops that supplied them with their materials, were to be found over much of Merseyside, for example in Bootle, Huyton, Waterloo, Garston, and Birkenhead and its suburbs, the centre of the dress and fashion world was, and remained, the centre of Liverpool: Lord Street, Church Street, Ranelagh Street, and, in particular, Bold Street. An article in the Jubilee Issue of the *Liverpool Review* of 14 June 1887 makes this point. 'The supremacy of Bold Street as a fashionable thoroughfare for the feminine pastime of 'shopping' is so nearly contemporaneous with the Victorian Era that it might appropriately celebrate a Jubilee of its own.' *(4)* By 1899, there are 50 entries in *Gore's Directory* for firms or persons engaged in some branch or other of the clothes trade, from the big 'Fashion Houses' of T & S Bacon, Cripps, Sons & Co and De Jong et Cie, via numerous drapers, shoe shops, milliners, dressmakers, glovers, furriers, to 'Wheeler & Wilson, Sewing Machine Mfrs.' In 1924 there are 55 such entries, and over two-thirds of the shops on the west side of the street are occupied by such businesses.

8

Liverpool in 1980 has no special claim to be a fashion or dressmaking centre. There are many dress shops, but nearly all belong to large national chains, and sell the same clothes as can be bought in any other city in the country. There are only a handful of professional dressmakers left, mostly to be found teaching in Training Colleges or Adult Education Centres. Hardly a remnant is to be found of the once-numerous 'Silk Mercers and Lacemen.' In some cases the department stores they developed into are still there, but not selling silks, or lace, instead, polyester fabrics and Courtelle. Bold Street, once called the 'Bond Street of the North', now has only the vestigial remains of the great fashion and dress industry that was her glory for almost 100 years. Bold Street today, interestingly, seems more interested in adorning the minds than the persons of its customers; it is becoming a street of bookshops.

Chapter 2
Victorian Dressmakers

IF seventy-seven milliners and dressmakers seems a large number for Liverpool to support in 1827, it must be remembered that their potential clientele came from quite a large area of rural SW Lancashire, as well as from within the town boundary. Villages such as Crosby, Sefton, Huyton and Woolton, later to be swallowed up by Liverpool as suburbs, then probably would not have been able to offer more than a plain seamstress and their inhabitants would have gone to Liverpool if they wanted anything at all stylish. The earliest dress with a known Merseyside provenance in the collections of Merseyside County Museums is one from such a rural background; a dress of fashionable printed challis, dating from about 1837 to 1839, and worn by a member of a farmer's family of Church Lane, Netherton *(plate 1)*. This is skilfully made, fully lined, with a boned bodice and a very fine, even line of piping outlining every bodice edge and seam, so it seems likely it was made by a town dressmaker. The owner would have had easy access to either Liverpool or Ormskirk, as a regular stage coach service ran along the Liverpool-Ormsirk-Preston road, now the A59. It would also have been possible to travel to Liverpool by canal from Netherton, as there was a regular packet service along the Leeds and Liverpool canal; the trip from Liverpool to Old Roan took two hours.

An examination of the addresses of the Liverpool milliners and dressmakers in 1827 reveals that they were all clustered round the present City Centre area *(Map A)*, in the main occupying streets that had been fashionable for the 'gentry' to reside in the late 18th century, such as Mount Pleasant, Islington and Duke Street, but from which the former occupants had moved on to the newer and smarter terraces and villas of Everton, Abercromby Square and Toxteth Park. Throughout the 19th century this pattern can be seen, the dressmakers and other similar 'service' trades occupying the fringes of the smart residential areas, near their clients but yet not presuming to be on a social level with them. Another, and probably more important reason for the location of the dressmaking trade at this date, is the necessity of being near the supply of materials, threads and trimmings, the suppliers of which were to be found in Church Street, Bold Street, Whitechapel, Byrom Street and some of the streets adjoining.

There was considerable specialisation in the retail side of the textile trade in the early 19th century. Nowadays, one would expect to be able to obtain all types of dress material at one shop; in 1827, however, the trade was generally divided between woollen merchants, who would sell all types of wool cloth and suitings; linen drapers, who would sell linens, cottons, and usually hosiery, haberdashery and trimmings as well; and silk mercers, who dealt in fine silks, muslins, gauzes

Plate 1. Dress of printed challis, made for a member of a farming family from Netherton near Liverpool 1837-9.

and lace, the smartest and costliest end of the trade. It is a measure of the size and importance of Liverpool's dressmaking industry that there was business enough for eighteen silk mercers in 1827, fifteen of which had premises in Church Street and Bold Street.

Unfortunately no local writer has left us a picture of a Liverpool dressmaking establishment in the early or mid-19th century, either factual or fictionalised, but it is probably safe to assume that they would not differ greatly from those in other Northern industrial towns which were rapidly expanding in a similar manner. Mrs Gaskell, in her novel *Mary Barton* published in 1848, describes life in working-class Manchester, and the two aspects of the dressmaking trade portrayed there would probably have closely paralleled conditions in Liverpool at the same date. Mary Barton, the daughter of a weaver, though unusually pretty and 'refined' for her background, wished to obtain a place as a dressmaker's apprentice, and having found that the 'first establishments' asked high premiums, she lowered her ideas and 'engaged herself — to a certain Miss Simmonds, milliner and dressmaker, in a respectable little street leading off Ardwick Green, where her business was duly announced in gold letters on a black background, enclosed in a bird's-eye maple frame, and stuck in the front parlour window; where the workwomen were called her 'young ladies', and where Mary was to work for two years without any remuneration, on consideration of being taught the business; and where afterwards she was to dine and have tea, with a small quarterly salary (paid quarterly, because this was so much more 'genteel' than weekly), a *very* small one, divisible into a minute weekly pittance. In summer, she was to be there by six, bringing her day's meals during the first two years; in winter she was not to come until after breakfast. Her time for returning home at night must always depend on the quantity of work Miss Simmonds had to do'. 'And', we are told, 'Mary was satisfied', though one would think she had little cause to be; still, it was cleaner, probably pleasanter, and certainly more genteel than the other alternatives, factory work or domestic service.

It is disappointing that Mrs Gaskell gives us only one other glimpse of Miss Simmonds's establishment, as she is likely to have had first-hand knowledge of such places, from both the customer's and the work girls' point of view. We can gather by implication, however, that the house was a small terraced house, the front parlour was used as a showroom and fitting room, and the back room as a workroom. There seem to have been at least half-a-dozen 'young ladies', all the sewing at this date still having to be done by hand. We take leave of Miss Simmonds's with a description of the scene on the morning after the murder of Henry Carson, who had been an admirer of Mary's.

'Miss Barton! as I live, dropping tears on that new silk gown of Mrs Hawkes'! Don't you know they will stain, and make it shabby for ever? Crying like a baby, because a handsome young man meets with an untimely end. For shame of yourself, Miss. Mind your character and your work if you please. Or, if you must

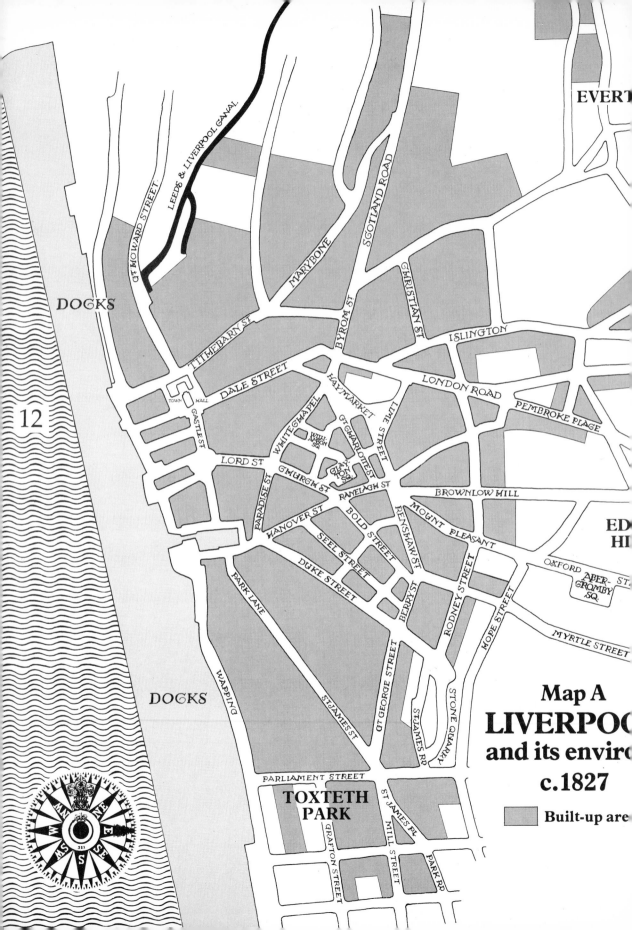

EVERT

DOCKS

LEEDS & LIVERPOOL CANAL.

GT HOWARD STREET

MARYBONE

SCOTLAND ROAD

CHRISTIAN ST

ISLINGTON

TITHEBARN ST

BYROM ST

LONDON ROAD

PEMBROKE PLACE

DALE STREET

TOWN HALL

CASTLE ST

HAYMARKET

LIME STREET

WHITECHAPEL

WILL. SON SQ

GT CHARLOTTE ST

GT CHARLOTTE ST

CLAY TON SQ.

12

LORD ST

CHURCH ST

RANELAGH ST

BROWNLOW HILL

PARADISE ST

HANOVER ST

BOLD STREET

RENSHAW ST

MOUNT PLEASANT

ED
HI

SEEL STREET

DUKE STREET

BERRY ST

RODNEY STREET

HOPE STREET

OXFORD ST
ABER-
CROMBY
SQ.

PARK LANE

GT GEORGE STREET

ST JAMES ST

ST JAMES RD

STONE QUARRY

MYRTLE STREET

DOCKS

WAPPING

Map A
LIVERPOO
and its enviro
c.1827

Built-up are

PARLIAMENT STREET

**TOXTETH
PARK**

ST JAMES PL

MILL STREET

GRAFTON STREET

PARK RD

311

cry' (seeing her scolding rather increased the flow of Mary's tears, than otherwise), 'take this print to cry over. That won't mark like this beautiful silk' rubbing it, as if she loved it, with a clean pocket-handkerchief, in order to soften the edges of the hard round drops.

Mary took the print, and naturally enough, having had leave given her to cry over it, rather checked the inclination to weep.'

In contrast to Mary, who in spite of her 'minute weekly pittance' is well off with her regular job in Miss Simmonds's workroom, there is her neighbour, Margaret Legh, 'who does plain-work, and now and then a bit in the dressmaking line'. What work she can get she does at home, and one evening she goes to ask Mary help her finish a job of work, mourning, 'as it must be in time for the funeral tomorrow'.

'I only got the order yesterday at noon; and there's three girls beside the mother; and what with trying on, and matching the stuff (for there was not enough in the piece they chose first), I'm above a bit behindhand. I've the skirts all to make, I kept that work till candlelight; and the sleeves, to say nothing of little bits to the bodies; for the missis is very particular.' While they work together on the mourning, Margaret breaks the news to Mary that she is going blind. She had been advised by a doctor to give up sewing, if she wished to save her sight, but she could not afford to do so. 'Plain work pays so bad, and mourning has been so plentiful this winter, I were tempted to take in any black work I could; and now I'm suffering from it.' Blindness was an occupational hazard that had to be faced by those who sewed for a living in the 19th century.

Studying *Gore's Directory* for 1851, the number of milliners and dressmakers in Liverpool appears to have doubled, from 77 to 146; and perhaps more significantly, the number of silk mercers has increased from 18 to 55 in twenty-four years, attesting to a growing demand for the 'beautiful silks' such as Mary Barton carelessly attempted to spoil with her tears. As by now the fashionable and/or wealthy families had moved still further from the town centre, to Princes Park, Fairfield or Wavertree, so the dressmakers followed them; addresses are now found in Mill Street, Toxteth; Myrtle and Grove Streets; Pembroke Place and Erskine Street. Bold Street and London Road, however, are still the centres of the trade, 28 businesses being listed in the Bold Street area and 17 in London Road and its immediate neighbourhood *(plate 5)*.

It is very tantalising not to be able to ascribe any of the several beautiful 'local' dresses of this period in the collections to a particular dressmaker; no system of labelling existed then. Unusually fine and well-provenanced examples are two silk dresses, a bride's and her bridesmaid's, worn by Mary Ellen Clare and her sister Eleanor, daughters of Thomas Clare of 3 Wavertree Terrace. Mary Ellen married William Kershaw in 1854 at St Mary's Church, Edge Hill but alas there are no records to tell us who made her dress of glistening white satin, very plain and virginal, with little ruffles of silk net at neck and sleeve edges as the only ornament *(plate 2);* or her sister's dress of hyacinth blue silk glacé with a tiny

14

Plate 2. Wedding dress of white satin, made for Mary Ellen Clare of Edge Hill, 1854.

matching cape trimmed with fringing. It is tempting to think that the Miss Clares might have patronised Maria White, 10 Grinfield Street, Edge Hill, the nearest dressmaker to where they lived, but it is just as likely that they would have gone further afield for such an important order, as they would have had a carriage at their command.

As Liverpool entered the second half of the 19th century, its growth rate accelerated and it took only fifteen years for her dressmakers to more than double again. In 1867 there were 334, and a particularly striking feature of the Directory list is that addresses were to be found all over Merseyside. A couple of dressmakers had set themselves up in Birkenhead by 1851, but by the mid 1860s they were also to be found in Claughton, New Ferry, Egremont and Seacombe, and on the Liverpool side in Bootle, Kirkdale, Waterloo, Everton, West Derby, Huyton and Garston *(Map B)*. Bold Street, which at this time was being largely rebuilt, could boast of 14 silk mercers, and among those were several names destined to become very well known indeed: Samuel S Bacon, John Cripps & Co, and Woollright and Co; 70 or so other similar shops could be found in the rest of the town centre, in the suburbs, and in Birkenhead.

Conveniently close to Bold Street is Rodney Street, and in the 1870s and 1880s this appears to have been a smart area for the dressmaking trade. Three entries appear in 1867, Mrs Ann Maria Motion at No 20, Mrs Eleanor Whalley at No 24, and 'Lamb and Freer, Millinery Rooms' at No 47. This has increased to eight by 1880, but by 1895 the medical and dental professions had monopolised the street, as they still do today. Mrs Motion is of crucial importance to this survey of Liverpool dressmakers in that she was the first (so far discovered) who labelled her dresses. From 1872 onwards, trade papers had carried advertisements for 'dress-bands, mantle and coathangers, woven or printed on silk' *(1)* which carried the maker's name and address. Dress-bands, which were sewn in at the waist of the bodice, also served to make the boned bodice back fit closely to the figure *(plates 3a and 3b)*. Mrs Motion had hers made of white twilled silk and cotton, stamped in gold: 'Mrs Motion, Modes & Robes, 14 Rodney Street, Liverpool' *(2)*. Presumably she felt her clientele deserved such an outlay, as some of the richest (if not the smartest) Liverpool ladies went to her. The Museum of London has a dress so labelled which belonged to Lady Walker, the first wife of Sir Andrew Barclay Walker, the brewer, who used his immense fortune (as was said at the time) to buy himself civic honours and a peerage. Lady Walker, who was Mayoress during her husband's two Mayoralties, 1873-4 and 1876-7, could certainly afford the best.

A group of dresses in Merseyside County Museums' collections, all from the Barrow family of Prescot, show an interesting instance of family loyalty to Rodney Street dressmakers. One of the dresses, a rich garnet-red satin and velvet, worn by one of the Barrow ladies marrying for a second time, has Mrs Motion's label, and therefore must have been made in the late 1870s, as Mrs Motion disappears from the Directory in 1880. Her business was carried on at 14 Rodney

Plate 3a.
Dress band, woven with the name of George Henry Lee & Co Ltd, Basnett Street, c. 1904.

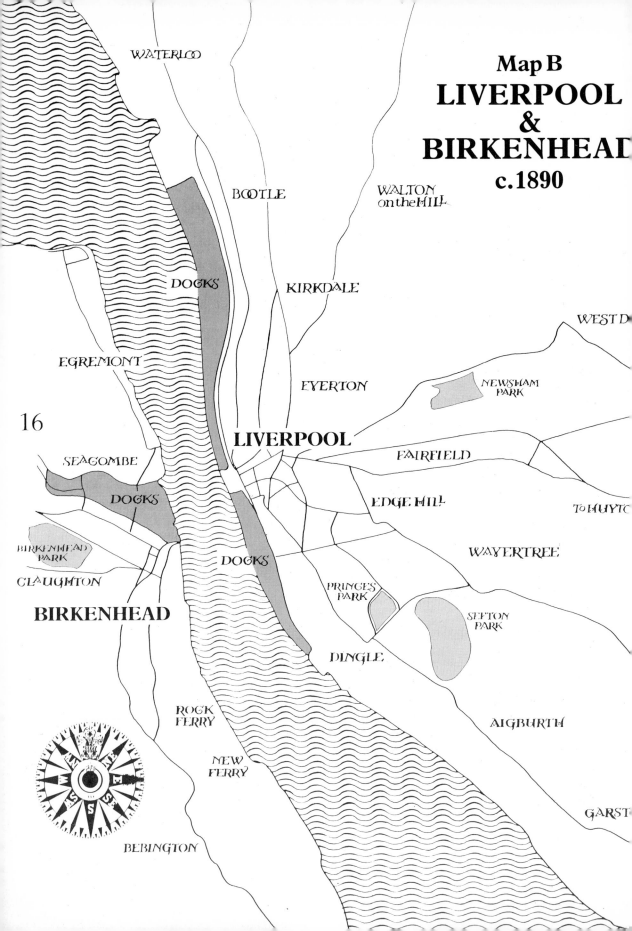

Street by Elizabeth Sherriff, and the Barrow family continued their custom with her, as the aforementioned twice-married lady's niece had her wedding dress and part of her trousseau made by her. Another Rodney Street dressmaker, Jane Merrick, who moved her business there in 1886 from 3 Oxford Street, counted among her customers Miss Nessie Muspratt, of Seaforth Hall, daughter of E K Muspratt of Muspratt & Co Chemical Works, later the United Alkali Company Ltd. Miss Muspratt married Egerton Stewart-Brown in Sefton Church in 1888, and Jane Merrick made her wedding dress of pearl grey satin brocaded in silver. *(plate 4)* To judge from the finish of this dress, Miss Merrick was a first-class dressmaker.

A valuable insight into the size and importance of the Rodney Street dressmaking establishments in the 1880s, and especially into the amount of stock and capital that could be involved, is provided by a printed handbill produced by George Henry Lee & Co in October 1893, in which they announce the sale of the stock of Miss Scott, 66 Rodney Street 'who for over 30 years carried on there a first class Private Dressmaking Establishment'. The 'somewhat extensive' stock of silks, brocades, velvets and laces was apparently selected by Miss Scott, personally, from 'the leading warehouses in Paris, London, etc . . .', obviously she did not rely on local suppliers. Many hundreds of yards of the choicest and richest silk fabrics are itemised, mostly sold as dress pieces or lengths of fifteen yards, at prices up to 4 guineas a yard for a 'White ground, gold and silver embroidered brocade' which was perhaps similar to the brocade of Miss Muspratt's wedding dress.

17

Alas, few of the several hundred Liverpool dressmakers in 1888 would be lucky enough to have clients with an income such as that of Lady Walker and Miss Muspratt. Probably typical of a great many of her fellow workers is the 'Cheap Dressmaker', subject of an article in the *Liverpool Review,* 17 September 1887. *(5)* In the latter part of this year the Review, a weekly paper with very liberal views, published a series of interviews with women workers at the lowest end of the clothing trade, at a time when some concern was being shown nationally about 'sweated' labour. The interview, the subject of which is not identified by name, or address, is reported in a factual and unbiased manner.

The article begins by describing the dressmaker's accommodation: the front room on the upper floor of a cottage, which served as bedroom as well as workroom, and where room had to be found for a sewing machine (hired, at 2/6d per week) and an apprentice. The interviewer asks what she gets for making a dress.

'That depends on the style of it. If it were a plain servant's dress, I would get three shillings. If there were much drapery about it, seven shillings, and if it was a very stylish sort of dress ten shillings. But what I mostly get to make are servants' dresses.' *(6)*

'How long does it take you to make a dress?' 'That is difficult to say, for it depends not only on the style of the dress but on the customer. Some people are never satisfied but come back again and again for alterations,

Plate 3b.
Dress band, printed with the name of Mrs Sherriff,
14 Rodney Street, successor to Mrs Motion, c. 1886.

18

Plate 4. Photograph, by Barraud of Bold Street, of Nessie Muspratt in her wedding dress, made by Jane Merrick of Rodney Street, 1888.

until you are sick of the very sight of the thing, and would like to burn it if you dared.'

'But suppose it's a plain dress and the customer not difficult to please?'

'I suppose about a couple of days would be sufficient in that case, if I did nothing else all the time. But there's a deal more stitching now even in the plainest dress than there used to be.'

'Have you any particular hours of work?'

'No, my hours of work depend on what I have to do, I begin when I get up in the morning and go on until I can't go on any longer.'

'Were you brought up to the millinery business?'

'No, I never served any apprenticeship to it, but I always made the dresses that were wanted when I was at home and I was thought rather clever at it, so when my parents died and our home was broken up, I took to it for a living.'

'How much do you think you earn one week with another all the year round?'

'About ten shillings I should think, but I can scarcely say for certain.'

A hard, depressing way of scraping together a living, is the impression that this interview gives, in spite of the subject's lack of self-pity, and her good fortune in having a kind landlady who assisted her financially when times were particularly bad. She would herself have known that she was lucky compared to some, as another article on 22 October 1887 reveals. This is headed 'Slop Workers in Liverpool. Grinding Poverty. Three day's work for Sixpence.' Slop workers were outworkers who made up cheap clothing (usually men's clothing) for shops. It was one of the worst forms of labour exploitation in the 19th century. The widow who was interviewed spent three days making up four waistcoats, for which she had to buy her own thread and needles, and for which she would be paid 2 shillings. Deducting the sewing machine hire and the cost of thread etc, this meant 6d profit for three day's work. For making up trousers she could get 5d each, minus the cost of thread, and she could get two pairs made in a day 'if she made do with very little sleep.' The highest price for shirtmaking was 2½d apiece, and find your own thread. Truly, making up servants' dresses for three shillings apiece was elegant, refined work compared with that.

19

B. COOKE AND DAUGHTERS,
(Successors to ANN BLAIN,)

RESPECTFULLY inform their Friends and the Public, that they have selected a neat and genteel Assortment of GOODS suitable for the Season, consisting of SWIES and ENGLISH PRINTS, MOUSSELINE DE LAINES, PRINTED MUSLINS, SILKS, WORKED COLLARS, FANCY HANDKERCHIEFS, &c., which will be ready for inspection on 3rd day, (Tuesday,) the 9th instant.

Also, an Assortment of BABY LINEN and CHILDREN'S DRESSES.

N.B. Family Orders for READY-MADE LINEN executed with care and despatch.

4, *DUKE STREET*, 5th month, 3rd, 1843.

SUMMER FASHIONS.
122, BOLD-STREET, FOUR DOORS ABOVE COLQUITT-STREET.

MRS. CUTTER respectfully announces her return from London with an elegant SELECTION of FRENCH and ENGLISH NOVELTIES, in Millinery, Flowers, Ribbons, &c., suited to the season, which will be ready for inspection This Day, (Friday,) and following days.

A large Assortment of Ladies' and Children's Straw Bonnets, in all the most fashionable Plaits, Boys' Hats, &c.

A Private Show-room for Improved French Medical Stays, to which Mrs. Cutter solicits the attention of the Ladies, and particularly Mothers.

MISS OLDHAM embraces this opportunity of returning her sincere thanks to those Friends who have so kindly patronised her since her commencement in the MILLINERY and DRESS-MAKING BUSINESS, and at the same time to inform them and the Ladies of Liverpool and neighbourhood, that she has been in London, and selected from the most respectable and fashionable Houses such modes and Fashions as are likely to be most prevalent for the ensuing season; she therefore most respectfully solicits their orders, trusting she shall be fully enabled to give satisfaction in the execution of any that she may receive.

Family Mourning strictly attended to.
No. 4, *MONUMENT-PLACE, LONDON-ROAD.*

MISS HENDERSON respectfully intimates to the Ladies of Liverpool and its Vicinity, that she has returned from London, where she has selected from the first Houses in the Metropolis, all that is NEW and FASHIONABLE in MILLINERY, MANTLES, DRESSES, &c., with every description of STRAW and FANCY BONNETS, which will be ready for inspection This Day, (Friday,) the 5th, and To-morrow, (Saturday,) the 6th instant.

Miss H. begs to decline sending circulars, in consequence of the uncertainty of their delivery.

MILLINERY-ROOMS, 41, *CHURCH-STREET.*

TRY MRS. HARRISON'S ELEGANT NEW BONNET, at 21s.
WHITE CHIPS, CUT TO ANY STYLE .... 25s.
PARIS BATESTE..8s. 6d.

THE MILLINERY at this Establishment is in style perfectly Parisian, at One half the Prices usually charged for Articles immeasurably inferior, both in style and quality. Mrs. HARRISON solicits orders and inspection, challenges comparison, and defies competition.

Observe—Mrs. HARRISON, 88, BOLD STREET.

☞ Mrs. HARRISON is always prepared to execute Wedding and Mourning Orders at two hours' notice.

MAGNIFICENT DISPLAY OF NEW SUMMER FABRICS,
IN DRESSES, FOREIGN LACES, ENBROIDERIES,
RIBBONS, BONNET MATERIALS,
FLOWERS, FEATHERS, SUMMER SHAWLS, AND
FANCY GOODS.
At 58. *BOLD-STREET,*
NEXT DOOR TO MR. DREAPER'S MUSIC BAZAAR.

JOHN LANGDALE respectfully announces to the Ladies his return from London, and is now offering an entirely NEW STOCK, which surpasses, in Extent, Taste, Novelty, Fashion, and Cheapness, any former Collection.

Milliners supplied at the Wholesale Prices.

LONDON AND PARIS FASHIONS.

R. M. BECKWITH, 72, BOLD-STREET, begs most respectfully to apprize his numerous Friends and the Public generally, that on THIS DAY (Friday) and following days his SHOW ROOMS will be opened with an elegant Assortment of MILLINERY, CAPS, and BONNETS, FLOWERS, FEATHERS, RIBBONS, &c., by him selected from the first Houses of Business, regardless of expense, to procure the first fashion of the day, together with a large Assortment of London and Dunstable STRAW HATS and BONNETS, too numerous for description.

Several first-rate ASSISTANTS WANTED, both in the Shop and Work-room; likewise several APPRENTICES to the MILLINERY BUSINESS.

Plate 5. Advertisements for millinery and dressmaking establishments, mostly in Bold Street, from the *Liverpool Mercury,* 5 May 1843.

Chapter 3
The Rise of the Ladies Outfitting Establishments

DON'T you think you would be better in a shop?' is a question asked in the interview with the 'Cheap Dressmaker' in 1887. This particular dressmaker, as it happens, did not, but nevertheless the Liverpool dress shops were now providing, by this date, a substantial part of the local output of ladies' clothing, both made-to-measure and ready-made, and a great deal of employment in their workrooms.

The rise to prominence of the 'Ladies Outfitting Establishments' had, however, been a gradual one. In 1827, almost nothing in the way of ladies clothes could be purchased in a shop; cloaks, and various accessories such as gloves and stockings, being the only exceptions. In 1845 Anne Hillyard & Co of 91 Bold Street advertised 'An elegant and fashionable assortment of *children's dresses* of the most novel manufacture and description always on hand. Also *ready-made linen,* suitable for individuals going abroad' *(1)(plate 6).* Linen in this context means underclothing, and the implication behind this phrasing is that whereas all really refined ladies normally made all their own underclothing, it *might* be permissible to buy ready-made if a large amount was needed in a hurry. Thomas Drinkwater at 27 Church Street also advertised 'Ladies' ready-made linen' in the early 1850s, *(plate 7)* but it seems that it was not until the 1860s that the many 'silk mercers, general drapers and lacemen' began to see that it might be worth their while to employ dressmakers to make up the various rich stuffs they sold to their customers' requirements, and thus make a profit on that side of the business as well.

The leaders in this field were both in Bold Street. John Cripps had set up a Shawl Warehouse at No 48 in the early 1840s *(plate 8),* to cater for the 'shawl boom' of the 1840s and 50s. In 1849 he moved to 12 and 14 Bold Street, and advertised himself in *Gore's Directory* as 'The Largest Shawl Establishment in the United Kingdom.' Presumably realising, however, by the early 1860s that shawls were on the wane, he looked for other specialities, and in 1867, resplendent with a new cast iron and plate-glass facade to his shop, he was able to advertise 'Warehouse for Shawls, Mantles, Silks, Dresses, Millinery, Lace Goods, Furs and Family Mourning' and in smaller type 'First-rate dressmakers always in attendance to measure and take orders.' *(plate 9)* We here have the first proof in print that a retail shop was producing made-to-measure fashionable clothes, and setting up a workroom and employing staff for the same. Further up Bold Street at Nos 81-85 Samuel Bacon implied that he was doing likewise, and resorting to French to make his creations seem more chic. 'Bacon, Samuel S, Silk Mercer, Lace Importer, Magazin des Modes et Robes' *(2).* In Samuel Bacon's case, such a development seems obvious and natural as his former partner, Henry Brown, who had been in business as a silk

Plate 7. Invoices from Drinkwater's of 27 Church Street,
(a) dating from c. 1868 and
(b) dated April 1877.

(a)

22

Plate 6. Advertisement for Anne Hillyard & Co,
Millinery and Baby Linen Warehouse,
from Gore's Directory, 1845.

(b)

MAISON DE LYON,

48, BOLD-STREET,

TWO DOORS BELOW CONCERT STREET

JOHN CRIPPS and CO.

Shawl Manufacturers

AND

CLOAKMEN.

J. C. and Co. have the honour of informing the Nobility, Gentry, and Strangers, that they have at all times an extensive and superior Stock of

SHAWLS, MANTLES, AND CLOAKS,

GOT UP IN THE VERY FIRST STYLE OF FASHION.

Every Article contained in this Warehouse (except Foreign Goods) are of their own *bonâ fide* production, thereby enabling them to offer many advantages to the Public, to be had at no other House.

The handsome manner in which the Public have responded to their endeavours, places them at the head of every Establishment of the kind in these dominions, and gives an impulse to their exertions to maintain that superiority.

STRANGERS AND VISITERS

WILL FIND

MAISON DE LYON

OF THE UTMOST IMPORTANCE, THE PROPRIETORS HAVING

AT COMMAND

THE LARGEST & CHEAPEST STOCK

IN THE KINGDOM.

The characteristic features in this Concern are
SMALL PROFITS, NO CREDIT,
AND NO DEVIATION FROM THE MARKED PRICE.

UPWARDS OF FIVE HUNDRED

TRAVELLING AND CARRIAGE CLOAKS

At all Seasons.

SHAWL AND MANTLE HOUSE,

48, Bold-street, near the Music-hall,

LIVERPOOL.

Plate 8. Advertisement for J Cripps & Co.,
Shawl and Mantle House, 48 Bold Street,
from *Gore's Directory*, 1845.

ONE OF THE LARGEST SHAWL WAREHOUSES IN THE UNITED KINGDOM

JOHN CRIPPS AND CO.

14 & 16, BOLD STREET, LIVERPOOL,

WAREHOUSE FOR

SHAWLS, MANTLES, SILKS, DRESSES, MILLINERY

LACE GOODS, FURS and FAMILY MOURNING.

FIRST-RATE DRESSMAKERS ALWAYS IN ATTENDANCE TO MEASURE AND TAKE ORDERS.

WEDDING AND MOURNING ORDERS WELL EXECUTED.

Plate 9. Advertisement for J Cripps & Co.,
14 & 16 Bold Street, from *Gore's Directory*, 1867.

23

24

Plate 10. Wedding dress, grey corded silk, made by Wm. Henderson & Sons, Church Street, for Eleanor Kershaw, 1886.

mercer at 83 Bold Street since the 1830s, had had a wife or sister Isabella Brown, who carried on a dressmaking and millinery business next door at No 81 *(3)*.

In the next decade the majority of the other silk mercers and high-class drapers followed suit and set up dressmaking deparments, usually situated on the upper floors of their town centre shops. The firm of George Henry Lee & Co of Basnett Street (founded by George and Henry Lee in 1853 as a Straw Bonnet Warehouse) were producing garments and millinery with their labels inside by 1880, as the Museum has on loan a cream felt hat so labelled, trimmed with purple satin and ostrich plumes, worn by Miss Elizabeth Jackson of Toxteth at her marriage in that year. Frisby, Dyke & Co of 58-66 Lord Street, founded in 1850, described themselves as 'Drapers and Outfitters' in 1880, and obviously drew their customers from a wide area, judging by the provenance of the only Frisby Dyke labelled dress in the Museums' collections. It was the wedding dress of a Miss Newport, a yeoman farmer's daughter from Delamere, Cheshire. According to her daughter, her mother and her sisters 'came to Liverpool to shop, and to the dentist in Rodney Street' a distance of at least 30 miles. William Henderson & Sons, of 11-13 Church Street, made the wedding dress of Miss Eleanor Jane Kershaw of Grassendale Park, for her marriage in 1886, *(plate 10)* and also a handsome elaborately-draped black satin skirt, decorated with jet beads, worn by the bride's aunt on the same occasion. *(4)* Hendersons did not intend their label to go unnoticed. It is 6 inches long, woven in yellow on black, and announces 'Wm Henderson & Sons, Church Street, Liverpool, Costumiers and General Drapers' within a scroll.

On the other side of the Mersey, the area around Hamilton Square, Birkenhead, was developing as a fashion centre for the local gentry. A pretty pale blue silk brocade and cashmere evening dress, possibly her first, was made for a Miss Stringer by Heald and Batchelor, of 67 & 69 Hamilton Street, about 1883 *(plate 11)*.

By the mid 1890s, these shops and other lesser ones were producing a very large amount of bespoke clothes of all kinds, for day or evening, indoors and outdoors, and fiercely competing with each other. There seems already, however, to have been established a social hierarchy. T & S Bacon, as the firm was now called, having moved to new premises at 62 Bold Street, was the most exclusive and expensive. The ladies of the big shipowning families, such as the Holts and the Hollands, had dresses made there *(plate 12)*. Cripps, Sons & Co were their close rivals, and possibly they had the edge over Bacon's when it came to the younger set, as the Holland daughters, Catherine, Elizabeth and Hester, had their evening frocks made there — the ones they did not have made in Paris *(plate 13)*. Cripps also claimed that their 'specialité' was wedding trousseaux, and they had a large fur department. A third establishment in Bold Street was De Jong et Cie, founded as a millinery business in the early 1870s by an enterprising family of Dutch origin. By the late 1880s, however, they seem to have been fully equipped to compete with Bacons and Cripps as fashionable dressmakers. A more specialist

Plate 11. Evening dress, pale blue brocaded silk and cashmere, made by Heald & Batchelor, 67 & 69 Hamilton Street, Birkenhead. c. 1883.

Plate 12. Day dress, sage green crepon, made by T & S Bacon, Bold Street for a member of the Holland family of Carnatic Hall, c. 1894.

establishment, W Creamer & Co, Furriers, at 56 Bold Street, were able to give a particularly distinguished air to their advertising. 'W Creamer & Co Furriers (By Special Appointment) to the Queen and to HRH The Princess Beatrice.' *(5)*

George Henry Lee & Co was undoubtedly the smartest dress establishment outside Bold Street, and in terms of staff and turnover, the largest of all. The original premises, 20 and 22 Basnett Street, had been greatly extended in the 1870s and 1880s, and by 1899 the firm owned 20-36 Basnett Street and 25-27 Leigh Street, and employed over 1,100 warehouse, shop and workroom staff. (In comparison, Cripps, Sons & Co employed 200.) Lee's could also boast of the honour of having provided Liverpool's first 'Shopkeeper Mayor', in the person of Mr T W Oakshott, the Senior Partner, in 1887/8. More garments seem to have survived with Lee's label in than from any other Liverpool shop, and the wearers seem to have been the wives and families of business and professional men, such as Mrs John Bewley, whose husband was a chartered accountant (J Bewley & Sons) and who ordered an evening dress of pale pink satin brocaded with tulips for a Town Hall reception in 1893 *(plate 14)*. The other shops, Frisby Dykes, Hendersons, Woollright & Co, do not seem to have managed to attain quite the same social cachet as the Bold Street shops and Lee's; they could not claim to be exclusive, but made a point of offering instead solid, middle-class, value for money. Sales at these shops, a regular feature from the 1880s onwards, were extremely popular and widely-advertised events *(plate 15b)*.

In order to provide this 'bespoke' fashion service for their customers as economically as possible, these shops would have employed dressmaking staff at very low wages, and probably expected them to work in inadequate and overcrowded workrooms. Some shops provided lodgings for their staff over the workrooms, a 'benefit' of doubtful value to them. Miss Stevenson Jones, whose reminiscences of Liverpool at the turn of the century were recorded by Museum staff in 1968, recalled that her father had seen the workgirls' dormitories on the top floor of Woollrights in Bold Street. When the 'Cheap Dressmaker' interviewed in the 'Liverpool Review' article was asked whether she would not be better in a shop, her answer was:

'No. They will only take women in shops — I mean shops that it would be worth going to — who have been regularly trained to the business and are clever in every branch of it. If they are clever in cutting out, fitting and draping they can make a good income. I don't know enough to do that'.

'But there must be a great deal of work to be done in a shop besides what you mention.'

'Oh yes, but it is done mostly by girls who are very badly paid. But as they are nearly all girls who are living at home, what they earn is not of much consequence except for pocket money. It's girls of that sort, with parents who are able to keep them, who make it so hard for poor women to earn a living.' There was obviously a big differential in pay between the senior staff, the cutters and fitters, and the

29

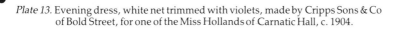

Plate 13. Evening dress, white net trimmed with violets, made by Cripps Sons & Co
of Bold Street, for one of the Miss Hollands of Carnatic Hall, c. 1904.

30

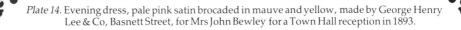

Plate 14. Evening dress, pale pink satin brocaded in mauve and yellow, made by George Henry Lee & Co, Basnett Street, for Mrs John Bewley for a Town Hall reception in 1893.

ON RETIREMENT FROM BUSINESS,

S. S. BACON,

52, BOLD-STREET, LIVERPOOL,

ANNOUNCES THE

SALE OF HIS ENTIRE STOCK,

OF THE VALUE OF £30,000.

Of this Amount nearly £10,000 Consists of

SILKS (BLACK AND COLOURED), SATINS, AND VELVETS,

The Remainder in

MANTLES AND CLOAKS, LADIES' AND CHILDREN'S OUTFITTING, MILLINERY, COSTUMES, SKIRTS, &c.. FURS, SHAWLS,

DRESS MATERIALS (Very Large Stock), REAL AND IMITATION LACES, RIBBONS, GLOVES, AND TRIMMINGS, HOUSEHOLD LINEN, SHEETING, DAMASKS, DRAPERY, &c., GUIPURE ANTIQUE (Real Lace) CURTAINS.

All the above including Black Dress Materials, Black Silks of the best manufacture, and Real Laces and Indian Shawls of unique quality and design, are offered at immense sacrifice and absolutely without restriction. The whole of this important and valuable Stock must be realised by the 25th inst., and a genuine and rare opportunity is thus given for the purchase of the highest class and most desirable goods in the trade.

TERMS: NETT CASH.

Catalogues on application.

3fe15

S. S. BACON,

52, BOLD-STREET, LIVERPOOL.

Plate 15a. Notice announcing the Retirement Sale of Samuel Bacon, Bold Street, from the *Liverpool Courier,* 15 February 1888. The firm subsequently traded under the name T & S Bacon.

FRISBY, DYKE, & CO.'S

ANNUAL STOCK-TAKING SALE

IN THE

COSTUME DEPARTMENT.

ALL THIS SEASON'S COSTUMES MUST BE CLEARED PREVIOUS TO STOCK-TAKING,

LADIES MAY THEREFORE RELY ON GETTING SOME GENUINE BARGAINS.

With a few exceptions the Bodices are unmade, but are completed at a small additional cost, and a good fit is guaranteed.

Useful Material Costumes in Tweeds and Plain Dress Cloth, 19/11: usual price 29/5.

Foule, Tweed, Beige, and other useful Dresses at 26/9; usual price 37/6 and 42/-.

Scotch Homespun Dresses, small checks, suitable for present and early spring wear, 29/6; usual price 45/-

Navy Serge Costumes, made from the All-Wool Stabilis Dyed Serges, and thoroughly shrunk, 29/6; worth 2 guineas.

At 32/6, 35/6, and 39/6, a large lot of Fashionable Costumes, composed of Plain Dress Cloths, Stripe Tweeds, Stripe and Plain Combinations, and other useful Dresses, at less than half-price.

45/-, 49/6, and 55/-.—In these prices will be the better class of Costumes, which have been double the price, and in many cases more.

BLACK COSTUMES.

Black Cachemire Costumes, 25/9 to 65/-.

Black Indian Cachemire Costumes, 29/6; usually sold at 2 guineas.

Black Serge Costumes, 29/6; worth 2 guineas.

Black Costumes, with silk, velvet, and crape trimming, all at sale prices.

The remaining Stock, consisting of about 20 Ball and Evening Costumes, at half-price.

Black Silk, Satin Merveilleux, Faille Francais, Black Lace, and Lace and Satin Costumes, Bodices unmade.

Black Lace Costumes, satin kilt, 47/6 for 39/6
Black Lace Costumes, satin kilt, 55/- for 45/-.
Black Lace Costumes, satin kilt, 59/6 for 49/6.
Lace Dresses, over silk and satin foundation, 55/-, 65/- and 75/-.
Black Merveilleux Costumes, 69/6 for 57/6.
Satin Merveilleux Costumes, 6 guineas for 4½ guineas.
Satin Duchesse Costumes, 7½ guineas for 5½ guineas.
Satin Merveilleux Costumes, handsomely trimmed jet cord ornaments, 7 guineas for 5½ guineas.
Handsomely Trimmed Satin Merveilleux Duchesse and a [illegible]e Silk Dresses, at 50 per cent. under price.

Special Orders in the Costume Department at Sale Prices.

BLACK DRESS MATERIALS AND COMBINATION ROBES.

50 Pieces ALL-WOOL BLACK FRENCH MERINOES.

Regular Prices,	1/11½,	2/3	2/6,	2/11,	3/6
Sale Prices	1/6½,	1/9,	1/11½,	2/6½,	2/11½

100 Pieces BLACK CACHEMIRES.

Regular Prices,	1/2½,	1/4½,	1/6½,	1/9½,	1/11
Sale Prices....	1/-,	1/1½,	1/3,	1/6,	1/7½
Regular Prices,	2/6,	2/11,	3/6,	3/11,	4/6
Sale Prices....	2/1,	2/6	2/11½,	3/6,	3/11

50 Pieces BLACK INDIAN CACHEMIRES.

Regular Prices,	2/6½,	2/11,	3/6	3/11
Sale Prices..,.	1/11½,	2/6,	2/11½,	3/3

A large range of good class Fancy Black Materials in double width, all at Sale Prices.

50 Pieces Stripe Broché and Fancy Black Grenadine, 7¾d to 3/6, all at reduced prices.

BLACK COMBINATION ROBES. — Special Line—25 Robes, composed of All-Wool Indian Cachemire and handsome Stripe Velvet, 19/11; worth 2 guineas. Cachmire and Silk, Cachemire and Velvet, and a large variety of other Combinations in Black, at about half price.

500 Robe Lengths, "unmade," of New Fancy Black Materials, 21/6; regular price 37/6.

SPECIAL REMNANT DAYS IN THE DRESS DEPARTMENT, FRIDAYS AND SATURDAYS.

FRISBY, DYKE, & CO.,

LORD-STREET. d

Plate 15b. Sale notice for Frisby, Dyke & Co., Lord Street, from the *Liverpool Courier,* 15 February 1888.

sewing girls.

When it came to training, the system had changed little since Mary Barton's day. Girls started as apprentices and would work for up to two years with no wages or scarcely any, and often scarcely touching a needle. It was the apprentices' task to run errands, and Miss Stevenson Jones recalled: 'When you went into George Henry Lee's, or the Bon Marché, or Compton House (6), at the counters selling trimmings, sewing threads and so on, there would be umpteen girls there sent by the dressmakers to match reels of cotton or bindings for the garments they were making . . . People from the workrooms upstairs would come down with an order for the haberdashery counters . . .' They also delivered customers' completed orders, by Hansom cab if the client was of sufficient status, or by public transport if not. A lady who was an apprentice milliner just before the First World War remembered having to deliver huge hat boxes, and the struggles she had with them on the trams. The apprenticeship over, the employee would be subjected to a different sort of exploitation. Although sewing machines could be extensively used in the construction of dresses, an immense amount of hand sewing was still necessary in order to apply the many and varied types of decoration — beading, lace, appliqué — beloved of the fashionable Edwardian customer. *(plate 16)* Miss Stevenson Jones, though one of the customers, was honest enough to admit 'That close sewing was very bad for a great many of these girls, it was a wretched existence for them . . .'

Most of the ladies who came in their carriages to shop in Bold Street would not, however, have worried themselves unduly about the working conditions of the girls in the workrooms above. Shopping for clothes in Liverpool about 1900 must have been a leisurely and most agreeable way of passing the time. Miss Stevenson Jones described Bold Street as she remembered it:-

'The exclusive shops were there, Bacon's, Cripps's, De Jong . . . they had nothing showing in the windows at all . . . at Cripps, Bacons, and George Henry Lee's in Basnett Street it was the same, a brown gauze blind across with the name of the firm on it . . . All the shops had a man in livery at the door; he was usually there for years and years and knew everybody. If a lady arrived in a carriage he would help her out, and take her umbrella for her, and usher her out and call her carriage when she left. At these shops Mr Bacon himself would be there, and old Mr Cripps and his sons at Cripps's, Mr Oakshott at Lee's . . . the heads of the firms were actually there in person, making sure everything was properly attended to. They would keep their eye on things . . .'

'Now I will tell you what it was like buying a dress. At Bacon's, Cripps's and the other shops, they had yardage, tremendous quantities of materials; in Cripps the left hand side of the shop right the way in was lined with shelves with huge bales of silks, tweed, cloth, all sorts of materials, and they had men assistants there, because the bales were very heavy to move. Further back were the dressmaking people, and if you wanted a dress you would go and see them. Each year they had a

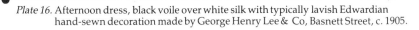

Plate 16. Afternoon dress, black voile over white silk with typically lavish Edwardian
hand-sewn decoration made by George Henry Lee & Co, Basnett Street, c. 1905.

certain number of model dresses, and they would show you these dresses. They did have at Cripps one or two girls who would slip on these dresses to show you what they looked like. The lady assistant might say, 'would you like the bodice so-and-so', or 'what kind of trimmings would you like?' And then you would choose your material; the young men would bring suitable materials for you to see. You had to be fitted, three times, or certainly twice, for that garment; first a calico fitting, and from that the material was cut and you had another fitting, and sometimes another after that. They did the same with children's clothes, I remember being taken up to the workroom to see the people who were making my party dress.'

Miss Stevenson Jones thought the whole process took about a fortnight, from the initial ordering of the dress to the final delivery; 'though if things were wanted in a hurry, it could usually be managed.' Orders for mourning especially had to be rushed through; all those shops had mourning departments which would carry a stock of partially-made up garments in order to be able to supply complete outfits in time for the funeral.

In all, it was a system designed to make the Edwardian lady customer feel very special and important. All that was required on her part was unlimited time, and quite a lot of money. It was not even necessary to attend the shop for fittings; if required, the fitter would be sent in a cab with the dress, for the customer to have her fittings at home. And if she was displeased with either the finished dress, or the quality of attention she had received from the shop staff, she could transfer her custom to a rival establishment. It was altogether a most undemocratic system, but it was supported by the workers quite as much as the customers, because the dress trade on Merseyside did offer a livelihood (of a kind) to a large number of women, and few other employments were available *(7)*.

34

Chapter 4

The 20th Century: Costumiers and Department Stores

DURING the first decade of the 20th century, the Liverpool dress world offered increasing variety for both the customer and the worker. In addition to the big dress shops and the smaller suburban dressmakers as sources both of supply and of employment, several wholesale garment factories were established at this date, and an increasing amount of 'ready-made' was available in the shops. The backbone of the ready-made garment trade, ladies' underwear and blouses, formerly made by outworkers at piecework rates, were now made in 'Manufacturies' such as that of Wm Lenton Ltd *(1)*, whose factory was at 202-204 Brownlow Hill, and who had retail shops in Cases Street and London Road. Other ready-made items of ladies wear available were cotton dresses, plain 'separates' i.e. skirts, jackets and blouses, suitable for servants and working girls, and mantles, capes and overcoats. Most of this output was aimed at the lower-middle class and working-class market, and was sold in the less 'classy' City Centre department stores, such as Lewis's, and in suburban shops.

In spite of this growth in shop and factory-made clothing, there was still plenty of work for the self-employed dressmaker, whether she rented a top-floor room in Bold Street, or worked from her home, a terraced house on the fringes of one of the affluent suburbs such as Sefton Park or Calderstones. Miss Stevenson Jones said with emphasis 'You only went to the Bold Street shops for the *special* things, the local dressmaker used to turn out the ordinary, everyday clothes.' Her family lived in Mossley Hill Drive and employed a dressmaker, Miss Gardner, 'somewhere beyond the end of Lark Lane' (9 Bryanston Road, according to Gore's), and also a Miss Jones, who had 'six or eight girls working for her in her rooms.' It was also possible to arrange for a dressmaker to come to one's house and make clothes there. 'We had one, a very nice Miss Thomas, who used to come for a week, and she would be able to make several dresses in this time, she was very clever at planning and doing things.' This system seems to have been particularly popular in the 1920s.

A constant source of income for the local dressmaker was, as it continued to be until very recently, the wedding dress. There were many Merseyside brides who preferred to forego the expense, and the parade, consequent upon ordering their wedding dresses at Bold Street, and therefore had them made and fitted in their own home or in their neighbourhood. A beautiful cream crêpe de Chine dress in the Museums' collections was made about 1903 by the Misses Parry, Wolseley Villa, Welfield Place, Dingle, for an, alas, unknown bride, but one of some social standing judging from the quality of the dress. Most of the considerable number

36

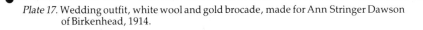

Plate 17. Wedding outfit, white wool and gold brocade, made for Ann Stringer Dawson of Birkenhead, 1914.

of wedding dresses of this period (1900-1920) in the Museum are not labelled. Of particular interest is the wedding dress of Miss Ann Stringer Dawson of Birkenhead, who studied at the Liverpool College of Art, and in 1914 married the painter James Grant. Family tradition has it that she designed her wedding dress herself, and it is certainly an original creation, with a gold brocade skirt forming a fish-tailed train, and a short overskirt and draped bodice of cream wool with borders of gold embroidery *(plate 17)*. The black and cream picture hat, with ostrich plumes, is labelled: 'Millicent & Co, Bold Street'. It is said that the outfit shocked some of Miss Dawson's conventionally-minded relations. In contrast, a very subdued, dainty ensemble was worn by Miss Lucie Musker for her wedding in 1917 at Walton-on-the-Hill parish church. Her high waisted pinafore-style, calf length dress is in navy velvet and navy chiffon lined with pink. The matching wide-brimmed navy hat is trimmed with tiny pink rosebuds *(plate 18)*.

Perhaps surprisingly, the First World War brought about very little change in this pattern. Although there was a much greater variety of employment available for women after the war, there was still plenty of demand for the local dressmaker, and large numbers of women earned their living this way. Bold Street became fuller than ever before of dress shops, dressmakers, milliners and other allied businesses. Some shops disappeared, notably Woollright & Co at Nos 18-26, which had been a drapery business since the 1820s; their premises were demolished in the early 1930s and rebuilt as the Gas Showrooms. Other shops expanded: Cripps, Sons & Co added No 12 to their existing shop at 14-16 in 1916. Yet others set themselves up from scratch, notably Sloan Ltd, which started as 'Mrs Ada Sloan, Dressmaker, 82 Bold Street' in 1915, became 'Sloan, Milliners and Dressmakers' at No 50 by 1924, and by 1930 'Sloan Ltd, Manufacturing Furriers, Dressmakers, Milliners, Riding Habit Makers, Sports and Colonial Outfitters, 48 & 50 Bold Street'. By 1940 the firm had expanded still further, acquiring the impressive address 42-50 Bold Street. Another important newcomer was the firm of Wetherall Ltd, which in the 1920s started business as 'Waterproof Coat Manufacturers.' Moving into the field of ladies' tailored coats and suits, and sportswear, Wetheralls acquired premises at 88 Bold Street in 1936.

If most of the Bold Street shops remained outwardly unchanged, the needs of their customers underwent considerable modifications in the post First World War period. The Society people, who patronised Bacon's and Cripps and some of the smaller costumiers such as Robina Robinson and Gladys Drinkwater *(2)*, no longer wanted trailing afternoon gowns, and garden party frocks, but tailored suits for racegoing (especially for Grand National Week, the highlight of the Merseyside Social Calendar), skiing and golfing outfits, cruise wear, luxurious silk lingerie, a certain amount of evening wear, and occasionally a court dress. An increasing amount of the work that was going through the workrooms of the long-established dress shops was alterations to last season's suits and evening dresses, re-modelling them for a more economically-minded clientele. It was not unknown for evening

37

Plate 18. Wedding outfit, navy velvet and navy chiffon over pink, made for Lucie Musker of Walton, 1917.

dresses to come back several years in succession for re-trimming.

Bacon's was still No 1 in Bold Street: their telegraphic address was 'Exclusive, Liverpool'. As a contemporary commentator put it: 'You paid to walk through the door. You really got the best, though.' Cripps, Sons & Co was also very expensive, their clientele was 'mainly business people' *(plate 19a)*. De Jong's specialised in fine lingerie *(plate 19b)*. Sloan's customers were 'mainly older people, with conservative tastes. The socialites didn't go there'. Another newcomer, Pacquin, at No 104, had 'the Jewish clientele'. The fashion buyers for these shops would go to London several times a year and buy a selection of model gowns, which would be shown to their regular customers by means of informal mannequin parades. A discreet card would be placed in the window saying 'Showing at 2.30 pm', and at the appointed hour the mannequin (one of the shop assistants) would come in and show off the model she was wearing to those who were present. Customers could then, if they wished, order copies for themselves.

As they had done for the previous sixty years, the Bold Street shops still offered a good deal of employment to trained dressmakers, and were considered particularly desirable establishments in which to learn the trade. Mrs Betty

Plate 19a.
Advertisement for
Cripps Sons & Co,
Basnett Street, 1930.

Sedgwick, who started as an apprentice with Bartram Orchard, 69 Bold Street, in 1930, remembers a good deal of the life and working conditions. Bartram Orchard's establishment occupied the ground floor of No 69, and largely consisted of an open-plan salon, from which various areas could be partitioned off with screens to make fitting rooms etc. The window was dressed every morning by the senior apprentice, who was 'showroom girl', with a gown and a hat. The apprentices still spent most of their time on errands, matching trimmings etc to fabrics, and Mrs Sedgwick did not use a needle for twelve months. Her special task was to follow the cutter, Miss Leaf, around, watch what she did, and fetch and carry for her. From Orchard's, Mrs Sedgwick moved to Gladys Drinkwater's at 5 Bold Street, a much larger establishment, occupying the 1st, 2nd and 3rd floors. Miss Drinkwater had a staff of about 20 and, apart from the apprentices, each had a specialised job to do. The key members of the team were the cutter and the fitter, then there were one or two bodice hands, one or two skirt hands, one or two coat hands, a sleeve hand, a collar hand, a cuff hand, and a finisher. In addition there was a milliner, two or three girls to do alterations, and several apprentices. A special table was kept for wedding, evening and court gowns, and everyone working on these would have to sit together round the table, sometimes a very cramped arrangement.

To achieve the right 'line' for the bias-cut dresses fashionable in the 1930s, the cutter never used a paper pattern, but went in for 'French cutting', ie draping and cutting straight into the material on the stand. Customers would choose designs from fashion plates in magazines that were acquired every month or so from France, showing the latest Parisian styles. The material having been decided

40

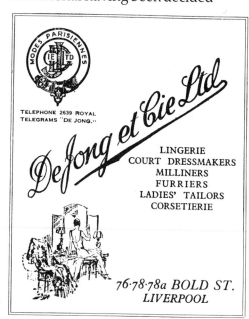

Plate 19b.
Advertisement for
De Jong et Cie,
Bold Street, 1930.

upon, the cutter would drape it on a stand and make suggestions. It was Mrs Sedgwick's job to make sketches of the ideas that met with the customer's approval, and to study her figure and memorise (but not note down, in case the customer saw) any figure abnormalities she might have. After the customer had gone, an apprentice would pad up a stand to her measurements, and the cutter would cut the material upon it. The skirt with its drapes would be cut first, and the bodice would be 'evolved' from the remaining pieces of fabric.

Life as junior cutter at Miss Drinkwaters did offer some compensations for hard work and long hours. Since she had the right figure for the current fashions, Mrs Sedgwick would be asked from time to time to attend some of the smartest of the local social functions, such as the Grand National Ball at the Adelphi, wearing one of her employer's latest creations as an advertisement. This would then be written up in the local press, and Miss Drinkwater would receive enquiries the next day, perhaps orders for copies in different materials or, in the case of a particularly affluent client, a request to purchase the original.

Bold Street could still afford to cling to its pre-war traditions of exclusive designs and individual service; the dress shops in other parts of the City Centre found it necessary to adopt a more democratic approach, and widen their appeal and the range of services they could offer, in order to stay in business in a world increasingly geared to machine-made goods for a mass market. Frisby, Dyke & Co were unable to keep up in the fashion race, the store steadily declined in the 1930s and the business and the building were totally destroyed in the 1941 Blitz. George Henry Lee & Co continued to be profitable, though the Model Dress Department in the 1930s was geared more to the mature woman with conventional tastes, and was thought 'stuffy' by Betty Sedgwick and her contemporaries. Having extensive premises, Lees were able to diversify into furniture, hardware and toys to boost their custom. Owen Owen's, formerly a drapery and haberdashery store in London Road, moved to a new building in Clayton Square in 1925 opening as a department store with its own Model Gown Department, which reputedly offered very good quality and value. The shop which seemed to adapt itself particularly to the atmosphere of the 1920s and 30s, however, was the Bon Marché, on the corner of Church Street and Basnett Street, which was completely rebuilt between 1920 and 1924, and spared no effort to promote itself as 'Liverpool's Modern Store'.

In the field of ladies' fashion, no less than three types of dressmaking service were offered (besides, of course, ready-made clothes), to meet all purses and requirements. The Model Gown Saloon on the second floor offered bespoke dressmaking in the traditional manner; the customer here would have to pay a minimum of 5 guineas, and prices then would vary with court gowns at 50 guineas being the most expensive. On the first floor was the Inexpensive Dressmaking Department (or INX as it was colloquially known). Here the customer chose a paper pattern, and the material she wanted from the fabric department, and this would be made up for her in the workroom. She would receive a bill, itemising the cost of material, pattern, thread, fastenings, trimmings if used, and a labour charge of 35/- *(3)*. This included a fitting, and a second fitting could be had if required at 5/- extra. Next door to the INX was the 'Cut and Fit' Department, which offered yet another service. Here the customer, having bought her pattern and material, could request to have it cut out and tacked up, and make an appointment to have a fitting. After it had been fitted she would take it home ready to sew. The charge for the 'Cut and Fit' service was 5/-. The assistant was allowed 1½ hours on each garment, 20 minutes for pinning and cutting out, one hour for tacking together, and 10 minutes for fitting. Considering the complexity of the bias-cut fashions of the 1930s, this service was probably well worth its modest cost. Henderson's and Lewis's also offered a cutting service to their customers.

In spite of the Bon Marché's versatility and readiness to adapt to changing needs and demands, it was the new arrivals in Church Street between the wars that indicated the way that the fashion, or at least the clothes world, was going. In 1925 the 'Fashion Store' of C&A Modes opened at 18 and 20 Church Street, and in 1930 Marks & Spencer Ltd acquired Compton House, the former premises of J H Watts & Co. Mass-produced clothes and the chain store had come to Church Street to stay.

42

Chapter 5
Postscript

BOLD Street was finished when Blacklers moved in during the War.' This is a conviction firmly held by some of Liverpool's older residents who shopped there before the 2nd World War, and while it is perhaps a little unfair to Blacklers, who moved there through necessity when their Great Charlotte St. premises were bombed, it is probably substantially true. The sort of rarified, glamorous atmosphere the Bold Street shops had created around themselves over a period of eighty or so years was not of the nature to survive such a radical vulgarisation. Moreover, in the years after the War the economic and social structure of Liverpool changed so much that most of the raison d'être for shops such as Bacon's disappeared. The female members of such of the 'County,' shipowning or cotton families as remained on Merseyside did not need such extensive or such expensive wardrobes, many of the social functions they had attended before the war had either ceased to be, or did not require the degree of formal dressing they had formerly. It was also far pleasanter to shop in Chester or Southport, towns which had not had their hearts torn out as Liverpool had, by wartime bombs and peacetime planning.

By 1948 De Jong's had gone, Sloan's gave up in 1954, Bacon's carried on in name until 1956 but since the war had only been a shadow of its former self. Jaegers moved into their premises at No. 52. Miss Drinkwater's establishment at number 5 survived until 1961. The last and longest-lived of the Bold Street fashion 'giants,' Cripps, closed amid widespread regret in 1972, partly because of falling sales but mainly because there was no one left in the Critten family, who then owned it, who wanted to run the business; it had remained for over 130 years a family firm. Wetheralls left Bold Street in the early 1970s, but still retain a Lord Street shop and their factory in Colquitt Street. Since the acquisition of Wetheralls by Baccarat in 1974 the company, as Baccarat/Wetherall Ltd, has successfully entered the international fashion market. The only Bold Street representatives of quality clothes today are Jaegers (who left Liverpool in 1967 but returned 10 years later) and Lucinda Byre, which opened in 1965 at number 4, and is one of the few successful survivors of the 1960s boutique fashion.

There was little work left in post war Liverpool for the self-employed dressmaker. Since the department stores and the chain stores could now provide clothes in every size and to suit nearly every taste, it was only for a very special outfit that the services of a dressmaker would be sought, and this usually meant her age-old standby, the wedding dress.

A beautiful example of a dressmaker-made wedding dress, representative of the last decade or so of the once so flourishing trade, is a dress made for Miss Nora

44

Plate 20. Photograph by E Chambre Hardman of Nora Wilton in her wedding dress
of white satin, made by Mrs E Wadsworth of Crosby, 1949.

Davies who was married at St Luke's Church, Crosby, in 1949 *(plate 20)*. The Museum was unusually lucky in that the bride was able to give, 25 years later, a detailed history of the dress and its maker. It was made by Mrs E. Wadsworth of Crosby, who was 'a real artist in her line,' she had trained with Frisby, Dyke & Co. before the First World War, and had been offered a job as cutter by one of the top London Fashion Houses but had been unable to take it because of chronic asthma. The dress material, a soft, white satin, was bought at Hendersons. Mrs Wadsworth made up a prototype, or 'toile' first, using a couple of sheets (one is reminded of Miss Stevenson Jones's Edwardian memory: 'First a calico fitting'), and from that she cut the dress. 'When it was finished she said it was her swan song, and the best thing she had ever made.'

Mrs Wadsworth, who was in very poor health at the time, knew her working life was at an end, and possibly she knew also that her particular art was dying. Her dress, made with so much skill, care and love, for Miss Davies, is worthy to be the swan song of the Liverpool dressmaking industry.

45

Notes and sources

Chapter 1

1. JANE AUSTEN: *Letters to her Sister Cassandra and others,* ed. R W Chapman, Oxford University Press 1952

2. ELLEN WEETON: *Journal of a Governess, 1807-1825* (2 vols) ed. J J Bagley, David & Charles Reprints 1969.

3. The term milliner in the 19th century was virtually synonomous with dressmaker; millinery meant all ladies' wear and fashion accessories, not just hats as it does today. The Trade Directories therefore always listed 'Milliners and Dressmakers' as a single category, as the dividing line was so vague.

4. *The Liverpool Review of Politics, Society, Literature and Art,* a weekly paper published from 1883-1904. (From 1878-1882 entitled *The Liberal Review of Politics, Society, Literature and Art).*

Chapter 2

1. Quotation from ALISON ADBURGHAM: *Shops and Shopping 1800-1914.* Allen and Unwin 1964.

2. Mrs Motion seems to have changed her address from 20 Rodney Street to 14 Rodney Street in the early 1870s. The 1867 entry in *Gore's Directory* reads: '20. Motion, Ann Maria, Milliner; Motion, James, Builder.' In 1879, the last time they appear, the entry reads: '14. Motion, Ann Maria, Milliner; Motion, James, Gentlemen.'

3. 'George Henry Lee & Co., beg to announce that on the recent retirement from business of Miss Scott, 66 Rodney Street, who for over 30 years carried on there a first class Private Dressmaking Establishment, they purchased her somewhat Extensive Stock of *Black and Coloured Silks, Brocades, Lyons Velvets, White Satins, Silks and Brocades, Rich Evening Silks, Woollen Dress Materials, Grenadines, Gauzes, Plushes, Rich Laces, Ribbons, Trimming Silks* . . . at a very considerable Discount from Cost Prices. The Stock throughout comprises goods of the finest qualities, selected by Miss Scott, personal from the leading Warehouses in Paris, London, etc., admirable taste having been displayed in th choice of colorings and designs, which include a the most fashionable shades and patterns.

It is not customary for GHL & Co. to buy Stock and they only do so under very exceptional circumstances, as in the present case. This is the first occasion on which they have ever bought a Private Dressmaker's stock, but the reputation h by the Vendor for so many years among the elite Liverpool, and the very excellent character of the goods in their opinion fully warranted the step taken.'

4. The equivalent in decimal currency of 4 guine is £4.20 A dress length would therefore have cos £63. To set against this, the average lower-middl class woman in the 1890s would probably have spent from £10-£15 a year on her clothes.

5. See Note 4 Chapter 1. The four *Liverpool Review* articles in 1887 are: Women Tailors, Aug 27; Cheap Dressmakers, September 17; Plain Sewing, October 15; Slopworkers in Liverpool, October 22.

6. The decimal currency equivalents for the pric quoted in this and the following extract are — 2¹⁄ 1p, 5d 2p, 6d (sixpence) 2½p, 1 shilling 5p.

Chapter 3

1. *Gore's Directory 1845.*

2. Samuel S Bacon had moved his business to 52 Bold Street by 1879. In 1888, upon his retirement the firm became known as T & S Bacon.

3. An advertisement in the *'Liverpool Mercury* May 1843 reads — 'Magazins de Modes 83 Bold Street. Mrs Brown respectfully announces her return from Paris, where she has selected a varie of novelties suited to the present season, comprising *Millinery, Dresses, Mantles, Shawls and Fancy Goods* which will be ready for inspec This Day (Friday) the 5th instant.'

This bride was the daughter of the 1845 bride, ~~ry Ellen Clare, whose dress is described in ~~pter 2. Her aunt, Eleanor Clare, wore the ~~esmaid's dress, also described.

~~he *Liverpool Review* 29 January 1887.

~~ompton House (J H Watts & Co.) was a large ~~pery, haberdashery and house furnishing store ~~ch faced the Bon Marché on the other side of ~~nett Street. It also had frontages on Church ~~et, Leigh Street and Tarleton Street. The ~~mises were acquired by Marks and Spencer Ltd ~~930.

~~he importance of the dress trade as the major ~~rce of employment for women is borne out by ~~es Cowper, recollecting her childhood in the ~~0s. *A Backward Glance on Merseyside* (privately ~~nted, 1948). 'At school I never surmounted the ~~iculties of arithmetic, which, strangely enough, ~~s deemed of far greater importance than English, ~~ the majority of the girl pupils would become ~~er dressmakers or milliners.'

~~apter 4

Gore's Directory 1912 lists: Lewton William ~~use and Underclothing Manufacturer, 202-204 ~~wnlow Hill (factory) 11 Cases Street and 215 ~~don Road (shops). In 1895 William Lewton's ~~nufactury' was at 33 & 35 School Lane, and the ~~wnlow Hill premises seem to have been a retail ~~pery shop.

~~Robina Robinson, Costumier, 31a Bold Street, ~~t appears in *Gore's Directory* in 1921. The ~~siness closed in the late 1930s. Gladys ~~nkwater, at No. 5 Bold Street, also started in ~~siness in the early 1920s but survived until 1961

~~Decimal currency equivalents: 35/- £1.75, 5/- 25p.

47